Shakespeare Without the Boring Bits

HUMPHREY CARPENTER

Shakespeare Without the Boring Bits

Illustrated by The Big i

VIKING

VIKING

Published by the Penguin Group
Penguin Books Ltd, 27 Wrights Lane, London W8 5TZ, England
Penguin Books USA Inc., 375 Hudson Street, New York, New York 10014, USA
Penguin Books Australia Ltd, Ringwood, Victoria, Australia
Penguin Books Canada Ltd, 10 Alcorn Avenue, Toronto, Ontario, Canada M4V 3B2
Penguin Books (NZ) Ltd, 182–190 Wairau Road, Auckland 10, New Zealand

Penguin Books Ltd, Registered Offices: Harmondsworth, Middlesex, England

First published 1994
5 7 9 10 8 6 4

Filmset by Datix International Limited, Bungay, Suffolk

Printed in England by Clays Ltd, St Ives plc

Set in 14/17 pt Monophoto Janson

A CIP catalogue record for this book is available from the British Library

ISBN 0–670–85533–2 (Hardback)
ISBN 0–670–85534–2 (Trade Paperback)

For Nigel Bryant
in gratitude

Contents

Introduction

I acted in a Shakespeare play before I ever saw one. It was *Henry the Fourth, Part One*, a school production. I played Francis, a waiter in the Boar's Head pub, and though my part wasn't very funny the audience laughed a lot, because my tights kept falling down.

After that, I started to watch the plays, both in school performances and at Stratford-on-Avon and in other theatres. I usually enjoyed lots of things in them, but there were always bits which sent me to sleep or which I really couldn't understand. When I was asked to retell the stories from some of the plays, I thought it was very important to leave out the boring bits – or rather, because very little of Shakespeare is really boring when you take the trouble to understand it, the bits that slow down the essential story.

I decided to have each play narrated by one of the characters from it, because I thought they would all have their own viewpoints, which might make the story come out quite differently. I began with *Romeo and Juliet*, told by the nurse, and *Julius Caesar*, told by Cassius, keeping the stories in their historical settings, because it didn't occur to me to change these. Then I happened to hear a wonderful radio production of *Twelfth Night*, directed for the BBC by Nigel Bryant, and I loved the way that, without changing the story, he'd set it in modern times. This gave me the idea of writing my own version of *Twelfth Night* in the form of letters from several of the characters, set at the present time. Then I was off!

Bottom in *A Midsummer Night's Dream* seemed to me a typical pub drunk, telling a long and unbelievable story in return for people buying him drinks. I suddenly saw that Shylock in *The Merchant of Venice* could be a modern City businessman, a tough banker, so I told that story from the point of view of one of his employees, Lancelot Gobbo, who speaks in a kind of accountant-ese (in my version, I mean, not in the original play. I played the part of Gobbo myself once, and found it very hard to get laughs from the lines Shakespeare had given him). *Macbeth* seemed to me a

Introduction

Shakespearian whodunnit or thriller, so I let Macbeth himself tell the story in the 'hardboiled private eye' style that American authors have loved to use since Raymond Chandler adapted it from Ernest Hemingway.

The Taming of the Shrew was a hard one; Kate's 'taming' is bound to seem pretty objectionable to modern audiences, and it wasn't till I thought about how her sister Bianca might have felt about it that I discovered how to tell the story. *Henry the Fifth* was easy; I'd decided to do it in TV news report style even before I reread the play – and then I was amused to discover that Shakespeare had had almost the same idea. The story of Henry's victories in France is told by the Chorus, an actor who speaks 'to camera' just like a television news reporter. As for *The Tempest*, this needs a little explanation. It isn't really a retelling of Shakespeare's play at all, but a short story suggested by it.

Writing this book has certainly made Shakespeare seem much more exciting for me. I hope that reading it does for you too.

Humphrey Carpenter

Romeo and Juliet

TOLD BY JULIET'S NURSE

Some people have said it was all our fault, me and Friar Lawrence. They say grown-ups shouldn't meddle in the affairs of youngsters like my poor little Juliet and her Romeo. But me, I say it was just bad luck.

They'd both be alive today, poor dears, if their families hadn't been fighting, fighting all the time. There must have been some reason why the Capulets – that's Juliet's family, where I worked – and the Montagues began quarrelling in the first place. But nobody can remember what it was. They'd been squabbling for years and years. So when the Capulets gave a party at their big house in Verona, none of them would have dreamt of inviting a Montague. Oh dear, no!

But one of the Montagues invited himself. I'm talking about young Romeo. A fine good-looking lad he was, and in those days he fancied a girl called Rosaline. He knew she'd be at the party, and it was a fancy dress affair, so he put on a mask and slipped in uninvited. The saucy boy!

He was spotted, though, by Lady Capulet's nephew, a fiery young fellow called Tybalt, who was always picking fights with the Montagues in the market-place. He recognized Romeo beneath the mask. And off he trotted to tell his uncle Lord Capulet that one of the enemy had gate-crashed! But my lord – I call him that because he was my employer, you see, dear – my lord had had a few drinks, and was feeling merry, and told Tybalt it didn't matter. And then what should happen but Romeo went and caught sight of my little Juliet, and fell in love with her on the spot.

I say 'little', but she was quite grown up really. Just a few days short of her fourteenth birthday. And there's many a girl in Verona was married by the time she was fourteen. But my lord, her father, didn't want her to rush into marriage. There was a decent young nobleman called Paris, who'd taken a proper fancy to little Juliet. But my lord Capulet told him he'd have to wait a couple of years before marrying her. No one asked Juliet what *she* thought about it. It was always the father that decided who put the wedding ring on their daughter's finger. Which is why Friar Lawrence was really being very naughty when he ... but I'm jumping ahead, dear.

Where was I? People say I chatter a lot, but I've not been the same since my poor Juliet passed away. And that was a few years ago now ... Oh yes, the party. Well. Romeo fell for her in an instant, and no surprise, because she was a proper little beauty. And she lost her heart to him too, there in the middle of the party. They were chattering away in a corner as if there was nobody else in the world. It was only later that he discovered she was a Capulet, and she found she'd fallen for a Montague. Head over heels in love with the enemy! Oh dear, oh dear.

After the party was over, I got Juliet ready for bed (she liked me to tuck her up, and say her prayers with her). She didn't tell me what had happened, but I sensed something was up. She went out on to her balcony for a breath of fresh air, and I heard her muttering, 'Romeo, Romeo, why are you called Romeo, why are you a Montague? How I wish you had another surname!'

And then I heard another voice, and, of course, I peeped through the curtain to see what was going on – well, wouldn't you? And can you believe it, Romeo had been wandering about in the orchard down below, trying to guess which was Juliet's window. And suddenly he'd spotted her on the balcony. And do you know, in a trice they were whispering sweet nothings to each other, without a care for anyone else.

Of course, I should have stopped it at once. But I pretended I wasn't seeing or hearing anything. Well, you're only young once, I thought, and I shut my eyes and stopped my ears, or at least I didn't listen too closely to all their lovey-dovey stuff. I gave them about five minutes before I called Juliet to come to bed. And do you know, in that time the two of them had decided to get married – the very next day! Nothing about asking Juliet's father's permission, oh, no. They were going to do it in secret.

Well, there was no stopping Romeo now he'd

found the girl of his dreams. While I was tucking little Juliet up in bed, and pretending I knew nothing about what was going on, he was racing along a path that led from Verona out into the country. Running like a wild thing to where good old Friar Lawrence lived in his hermit's hut. I say 'good', though there's some who argue that a man of God shouldn't meddle with magic herbs and drugs, the way the Friar did. But it takes all sorts, I always say.

Anyway, the sun was rising when young Romeo puffs and pants up the path. He finds the Friar picking his herbs, and Romeo tells him what's going on, and asks him to marry him to Juliet. Now, the old Friar, he thinks Romeo is really just a young hothead, because a few days earlier he'd been going potty about Rosaline. But it comes to the Friar's mind that if a Montague married a Capulet, it might make peace between the two families. At least that's what he said to Romeo, though if you ask me that was a pretty daft notion. He might have guessed it would only make things worse.

Meanwhile, back at our place, Juliet wakes, and sends me on an errand. Me, of all people, as if I was just any old messenger, and not a second mother to her. Her *real* mother, if you ask me, because I'd done everything for her since the hour she was born. Yes, she sends me puffing and panting out into the countryside, on a blazing hot day too. Can you believe it?

What's that? What was the errand about? Didn't I tell you? Oh, she wanted to see what naughty young Romeo had fixed up with the old Friar. And when I got back, phew, was I out of breath? And would she let me get my second wind, or have a nice cool drink? Not she! She wanted to know what I'd discovered, and she was too impatient to wait even a minute. What's that? What *had* I discovered? Why, you're just as impatient as she was, the poor little dear.

Well, what I told her was this: she was to slip off to Friar Lawrence's, as if she was going to church in the ordinary way. And when she got there, Romeo would be waiting, and the Friar would marry them.

And that's what happened. And did either of them invite me to their pretty little wedding? Not them, the naughty children. And as soon as they were married, they went their separate ways, but they arranged that Romeo would come and spend the night with Juliet in secret, at her house, climbing over the wall and up the balcony. And no one even told *me*, as if I had nothing to do with it!

Where was I? Oh yes. That's when the trouble really began. As I say, it was a hot day, a real scorcher, like we often had in Verona. And a noisy young friend of Romeo's, a really silly chatterbox called Mercutio, a harmless boy really, but a bit of a tease, he was fooling around in the town square. And what does he do but go and be cheeky to Tybalt, who was Lady Capulet's nephew (did I tell you that before?). And in the blink of an eye they'd drawn their swords, and Tybalt had stuck his blade right through poor young Mercutio. And by bad chance, at this moment up rolls Romeo, still starry-eyed from marrying his dream girl. He sees his best friend dead on the ground. Well, you can guess what happens next, can't you? That's right. Romeo's sword is sticking into Tybalt. So he's also dead, the poor young creature. Oh, it was terrible.

Now, the prince who ruled Verona was doing his best to stop the brawls between the Montagues and the Capulets, and in no time at all the officers of the law had rolled up. And quite right too. But it wasn't poor Romeo's fault, the quarrel. So it didn't seem right to banish *him* from Verona, to send him away and say he'd be killed if he was found there again. But I'm afraid that's what they did.

My poor darling Juliet was in despair when she heard, of course. It was bad enough that her darling husband – not that anyone knew he was her husband; you understand that, don't you? Where was I? Oh yes, it was bad enough that he'd killed her cousin Tybalt. But that they were sending him away, to another city, it was enough to make her sob her heart out.

I told you, didn't I, that Romeo and Juliet had planned to spend the night together? And who was I to stop them, knowing they were married in the sight of God. That's what I told myself. And, sure enough, Romeo comes to Juliet's room that night. Of course, I kept out of the way. But I couldn't help overhearing, when the sun came up and the lark began to sing, Juliet trying to persuade Romeo that it was still night-time, and the bird was the nightingale. Because, of course, she didn't want him to go.

But he slipped off, and hurried away to Mantua, which was the city they'd banished him to. And then what should happen, blow me down, but Juliet's mother, her real one, I mean, Lady Capulet, she breezes in and says that she and my lord have decided that Juliet will marry Paris right away.

My goodness, I was in a real sweat, wondering what we could do about that! And it was clever old Friar Lawrence who came up with the answer. At least, it would have been clever if they hadn't had bad luck ... I'm sorry, I'm trying not to cry, dear, but you must forgive me if I have a bit of a snivel for a moment. Pass me that handkerchief...

Oh dear, it really is too dreadful, I can hardly bear to tell the rest of the story. But what's been begun must be finished, I suppose. Where was I, dear? Oh yes, Friar Lawrence's plan. He'd made up this drug which, if you swallowed it, laid you out flat for a couple of days, so your heart stopped beating and everything, and folks thought you were dead. His idea was that Juliet should drink it, and, of course, her family would think the worst and, in no time at all, instead of marrying her to Paris, they'd be burying her. Except that the Capulets were too grand to be buried in the usual fashion. They always laid their dead ones out on slabs in an underground vault in the family chapel. So the Friar's idea was that Juliet would lie there on a slab, looking to all the world as if she was dead. And he'd send a message to Romeo, to tell him what was going on, and Romeo could slip back to Verona and rescue her.

Wasn't that clever? And it all worked out just as Friar Lawrence had said it would. Well, nearly.

Everyone screamed their heads off when they found Juliet looking like a dead body. And so did I, dear, because no one had troubled to tell me she wasn't dead. Oh, I've never seen such tears and heard such weeping. And in a few hours, she was laid in the family vault. All Verona was talking about it, of course. That was the trouble. Because the news that Juliet was dead had got to Mantua and the ears of Romeo before Friar Lawrence's message that she *wasn't* dead had reached him. And the poor boy was nearly struck dead by the news himself.

In no time at all, Romeo was back in Verona, still not knowing the truth, and he slipped into the chapel and down into the vault. And there was his beloved little wife, all cold to the touch on a stone slab. So what does he do but down a bottle of poison. Real poison. And dies. Really dies, I mean.

And then ... I'm sorry, but you're going to have to pass me that handkerchief again ... Oh dear. Well, you can guess what happens now, can't you? It's at this moment that my darling Juliet wakes up. And she sees him, her lovely Romeo, lying dead. And so she ... There was a knife, you see, a dagger, in Romeo's belt, and she used that to ...

I'm sorry, yes, I'm better now, thank you. It's just that I'll never forget my poor little baby lying there, covered with blood, next to her dead Romeo. Everyone was so shocked by it all that the Montagues and the Capulets stopped quarrelling from that day. So everyone says it turned out for the best. But all I can think of is my poor little girl ... Oh dear, I don't usually go to pieces like this. Put the kettle on, dear, and we'll try to think of something else to talk about before you go.

Julius Caesar

TOLD BY CASSIUS,
ONE OF THE MURDERERS

Did you know it was my birthday, Pindarus?
You're my slave and servant, you ought to remember the date. Well, there's a funny sort of birthday
present I want from you. Here's my sword. I
want you to kill me with it.

No, there's no hope for me now. No hope for
any of us. Why were we such idiots? 'Beware the
fifteenth day of March!' the half-mad fellow kept
calling out to Caesar, and the fifteenth was the
day we stabbed Caesar to death. But the man

ought to have warned *us*. Warned us that it was our *own* deaths we were plotting when we planned the whole thing.

It was me that started it. I just couldn't put up with the idea of Julius Caesar being crowned king – we Romans don't *have* kings – when I knew what a weakling he really was. I couldn't forget the day when Caesar had challenged me to a swimming race in the Tiber river, and then nearly drowned, so I'd had to rescue him. Or the time, on one of his famous fighting campaigns abroad – the ones that made him a national hero – when he'd had the flu and had been whimpering for a glass of water just like a little baby. The idea of such a person becoming the crowned dictator of Rome! I knew if they did make him king, he'd turn out a real bully.

Brutus was the first person I persuaded to join me in the plot. It wasn't easy. Brutus is an incredibly honest man, not the sort to plot an assassination, and he admired Caesar. Well, you couldn't help admiring him. Thanks to his brilliant handling of the army, Rome had become the ruler of just about every country in the world, or at least all the ones for thousands of miles around. Caesar was like a giant striding across the face of the earth, and the rest of us Romans looked like pygmies in comparison.

We didn't think that was right. It was all 'Caesar this' and 'Caesar that'. What about the rest of us? We'd all helped to make Rome great. We reckoned it was time we reminded the world of our existence. Caesar was starting to run Rome as a one-man show. *Not* a good thing for the likes of me and Brutus. And Brutus entirely agreed with me about that.

Casca soon came in with us, another powerful chap with friends in all the right places. I reckon what did the trick for him was the thunderstorm. That and all the creepy things that people kept reporting. Do you remember the thunder that night? And the lightning? You'd never seen or heard anything like it, had you? No, nor me. Nor Casca. He's a pretty cool sort of chap, but he reckoned the gods up there in the sky were angry with Rome about something. And it wasn't hard to guess what it might be. This scheme of Mark Antony's, Caesar's right-hand man, to crown Caesar king – the common people were all for it, the fools. But the thunderstorm gave some of us the idea that the gods were dead against it.

And there were some other strange signs too. Several people said they saw a slave running about the place with his hand apparently on fire, but it wasn't hurting him one bit. Then at noon, on a blazing hot day, an owl came and sat near the Forum, hooting and shrieking. I mean, an owl in the sunlight! Weird! It all added up to the feeling that something was very wrong in Rome. And *we* decided to set it right.

I wanted us to kill Mark Antony as well as Caesar. Well, I knew he'd make things pretty tricky for us if we left him alive. But Brutus was soft-hearted about it, said we shouldn't turn into butchers. So we agreed not to touch Antony. What idiots we were!

Of course, Brutus had to go and let his wife Portia in on the secret. Well, she'd spotted something was up. He couldn't sleep properly, couldn't eat his meals, kept muttering and sighing, and snapping at her when she asked him what was wrong. So in the end he told her.

Women, huh! What troublemakers they can be when a man's got a bit of simple killing to do.

Apparently Caesar's wife Calpurnia was having nightmares. She'd dreamt about a statue of her husband that had been stabbed all over the place. There was blood pouring out of it, and Roman citizens were bathing their hands in it. Strewth, that dream nearly did for us, because when she told Caesar about it, he agreed not to appear in public that day. Which was March the fifteenth, the day we'd planned for the killing. So when Decius, another of our bunch, turned up to collect him to take him to the Senate, he told Decius about the dream and said he wasn't budging.

Well, you have to take your hat off to Decius. He did a bit of quick thinking, and said the dream wasn't about Caesar being killed – quite the opposite. He said it was about Caesar's greatness: that he was a fountain feeding the whole of Rome with his nourishing blood. Brilliant. And Caesar was so conceited, he swallowed it whole. Whereupon Decius dropped a hint that if Caesar didn't come to the Senate that day, everyone might change their minds about crowning him king. Especially if they heard he was frightened by something his wife had dreamt! Well, of course, that did the trick. Caesar popped on his Senate robe and off he went with Decius.

So we killed him, just as we'd planned. Don't want to know the details, do you – you're squeamish about blood? You must be, Pindarus, old chap, because here you are holding my sword as if it would bite you, and all I want you to do is stick it in my guts as a birthday present. No, I am *not* joking. It's a perfectly easy thing to do. Didn't I do it to Caesar?

Yes, it was easy. Do you remember Cimber, whose brother had been banished? Well, he got on his knees in front of Caesar, just as the proceedings in the Senate were getting under way, and begged Caesar to change his mind about the banishment. And of course Caesar said no, and we all crowded round him, pretending to be pleading for Cimber's brother too, and we just pushed our knives in. All of us. And Caesar hadn't got time to say a word before it was over – except that the last person who knifed his guts was Brutus, and Caesar obviously couldn't believe that such a decent chap could turn killer, because he gasped out, 'You too, Brutus?' before he died.

Well, for a few moments we felt really good about it. We all kept shouting things like 'Liberty! Freedom! Tyranny is dead!' And we bathed our hands and arms in Caesar's blood just to prove to ourselves that he was dead. Just like the dream. And then Mark Antony walked in.

Everyone else must have run away, because there was just us, and Caesar's body, and Mark Antony. And, of course, we should have struck Mark Antony down then and there, like I'd said, because there was something in his eyes that spelt real trouble. But Brutus, the decent chap as always, let him say his bit.

And he said it brilliantly, the cunning creature. He didn't scream at us for killing the great Caesar, or call us murderers. Would you believe it, he shook hands with us, as if we were his best friends, and said he'd be grateful if we'd let him make a bit of a speech at Caesar's funeral. Well, I knew this was a bad idea, but that softy Brutus agreed to it.

You wouldn't think one man could change thousands of people's minds with a single speech, would you? But that's what happened. Of course, it was a tricky situation from the outset. The crowd in the Forum were hoping to see Caesar appear before them with a crown on his head. Instead, there was Brutus, getting up in front of them and telling them Caesar had been killed because he was too ambitious.

Then along comes Mark Antony with Caesar's body, the cloak Caesar had been wearing, and his trump card – Caesar's will. And he began to speak to the crowd. He didn't tell them we were murderers and criminals, oh no. He was far too clever for that. He kept saying that Brutus was a good man, and if Brutus said Caesar was too ambitious, he must be right. But he kept reminding them about all the good things Caesar had done for Rome. He held up Caesar's cloak and showed them where the knives had cut it. Then he read out Caesar's will and, blow me down, the cunning old fox had left all his money and his private gardens and everything to the people of Rome. That did it. The crowd went wild. And they were wild with us.

Not that I stayed around to hear that last bit. We were all on the run by then. We knew we'd blown it. The crowd were screaming about burn-

ing down our houses, but we were out of the city
by then. I'm afraid they caught and killed an
awful lot of innocent men, who they thought had
been in the plot with us.

Brutus had already lost his nerve, of course,
and then there was the awful business about his
wife Portia. After he ran off, she took poison.
Well, she'd been left alone in Rome, and Mark
Antony had got hold of Octavius, Caesar's heir,
and they were sending out the army against us,
so she reckoned it was all up for Brutus. And
when Brutus heard about that, it nearly did for
him, because he was very fond of her. But he was
coming to pieces even before that. He'd just been
accusing me of taking bribes – me! I've always
been as honest as the daylight! We'd been in it
together from the start, but now we were quarrelling like a pair of schoolkids, so we didn't have
much chance of winning the fight against Mark
Antony and Octavius.

But we've not put up a bad fight, have we,
Pindarus, even though I reckon we're outnum-
bered now? The trouble is, Brutus's heart hasn't
really been in the whole business since the start.
Do you know what he told me first thing this

morning? He says Caesar's ghost appeared to him last night, and warned him he'd see him on the battlefield, here at Philippi, and Brutus tried to put a brave face on it, but it upset him a lot.

I don't really blame him. I used not to believe in all that superstitious stuff, but I couldn't help noticing the eagles. Did you see them? A couple of fine birds that adopted us a few days ago. They've been sitting on our regimental banner, and letting the soldiers feed them from their hands. But this morning they flew off. And look up there – ravens, crows and kites! Birds of prey, hovering over *our* men. Well, they'll get their meat soon enough, I reckon. Mark Antony's men are advancing into our line, and I'm sure Brutus is dead already. He knew he was going to die today, because he shook hands with me, and said goodbye. Not the best frame of mind in which to fight a battle, is it? But there you are, like I say, I know now we were doomed from the start.

So, be a good lad and finish me off. It's the best birthday present you could possibly give me. I'm not going to have them take me alive and drag me through the streets of Rome before they do me in. A good Roman always dies on his own sword rather than letting himself be disgraced. Anyway, Pindarus, all those years ago in Parthia, when I took you prisoner, you promised you'd do anything I wanted if I spared your life. So you'd better keep that promise.

Come on, man. Just think of all those people who want my guts in return for Caesar's murder. This is the sword I stabbed him with. Do it for them.

I've shut my eyes, Pindarus, so come on, *get on with it.*

Twelfth Night

SOME LETTERS

FROM ORSINO TO OLIVIA

Most wonderful person in the world, heaven walking on earth,

Why won't you see me, or let me tell you how much I love you? I know your brother's death has made you miserable, but to shut yourself up and say you won't see anyone for seven years ... What can I say? I just sit here listening to music all the time, and thinking helplessly about you.

Don't keep your heart locked up against me any longer, darling.

With all the love in the world,
Orsino

Excuse handwriting – pissed as usual. Tell you what, old boy, you ought to marry my niece. Girlie by the name of Olivia. Very rich, inherited all her old man's dosh, then her brother died and she's shut herself away here like a bally nun, won't see anyone. What she needs is someone with film star looks, like you, old boy, ha ha ha, to come here and tease her out of it. Get here as soon as you can. I've got a few bottles that need drinking. Also there's a real saucy little thing that works in the kitchen, name of Maria. She could put life into old limbs, know what I mean, ha ha? Get here quick as you can.

Heard any good jokes lately?

Belchers

FROM VIOLA TO SEBASTIAN

Darling Seb,

I know you're probably dead – oh, it's awful – but the sailor who rescued me when the ship went down said he thought he saw you clinging to the mast, so I'm leaving this note at the port just in case. Besides, twins always know what's happening to each other, don't they, and I have a feeling you're all right, though goodness knows if we'll ever meet again.

The place where the lifeboat brought me is called Illyria, a pretty name, but it's quite rough, so when the people who rescued me offered me some men's clothes until my own were dry, I decided it wouldn't be a bad idea to go about disguised as a bloke. The first time I looked in the mirror, I thought it was you! People could never tell us apart when we wore the same things, could they?

Anyway, Count Orsino thinks I'm a teenage boy whose voice hasn't broken. He's the man who's given me a job. Rather dishy, actually, and he's the guy who rules Illyria, so I've done nicely for myself, except that things are getting a bit tricky.

Orsino has got the hots for a local beauty called Olivia. Bit of a rich bitch I thought she sounded till I met her, but really she's a sweetie, and she's in an absolute misery because her brother has just died (just like me and you – oh dear, I'm starting to cry). The first job Orsino gave me was to go and persuade her to come out of mourning and accept his offer of marriage, but she won't, and I don't blame her. The trouble is, *I think she's falling for me!*

Well, you can see why – I look exactly like you, you old heartbreaker, and she's not to know I'm not a guy. What *am* I to do?

Especially as I fancy Orsino something terrible. Shouldn't have told you that. God, what a mess.

All my love, darling Seb. You MUST be alive somewhere.

Vi

FROM SEBASTIAN TO VIOLA

Dear Twin,

Where on earth are you? When they rescued

me from the shipwreck and I got to this port, they said they'd seen someone like you being brought ashore, but no one knows where you've gone. I'm horribly afraid they're having me on, and you were really drowned. I'm leaving this note with the harbour master just in case you come back. Meanwhile I'm off in search of you.

Sebastian   X X X

FROM MALVOLIO TO OLIVIA

Report from Her Ladyship's Steward to Her Ladyship

Your Ladyship,

At 00.40 hours this morning, that is to say, at twenty minutes to one in the middle of the night, I was proceeding in a westerly direction from the entrance hall of your ladyship's mansion to the drawing-room, when I distinctly registered the sound of several persons in an advanced state of alcoholic inebriation. Pursuing these noises to their source, I came upon your ladyship's uncle, Sir T. Belch, reeking of drink like a public house. A young female person in your employment, a maid known as Maria, was seated upon your uncle's knee in a highly improper fashion. Also present at this disorderly gathering was a certain penniless knight, Sir A. Aguecheek, whom your ladyship's uncle recently invited to your lady-ship's house without your ladyship's permission. These persons were laughing coarsely at im-proper songs being performed for them in rau-cous fashion by your ladyship's resident come-dian, the fellow known as Feste. I informed all of these persons that they were keeping your lady-ship's household awake, and that if they did not immediately desist, I would be obliged to report the matter to your ladyship in the morning. In reply, the aforementioned persons addressed a number of remarks to me, the gist of which (let alone the specific words employed) I would not wish to stain your ladyship's ears by repeating. In laying this matter before your ladyship, I trust that your ladyship will judge that I have acted properly and with the true dignity befitting my position in your ladyship's household.

With extreme respects, your ladyship, I am
Your ladyship's Steward
Malvolio

Shakespeare Without the Boring Bits

We've got to do something about that pompous ass who ticked us off last night. You're good at handwriting – how about you faking a love-letter to him from Olivia?

T.B.

Hey, you gorgeous hunk, I may be an aristocrat, but don't think that means I don't fancy you, lover boy. Show me you care for me, honey-bunch. Don't put up with any cheek from my old relative, and as a special sign, get yourself a pair of stripy yellow fluorescent leggings, and wear them just for me. Boy, will you look sexy!

Hugs and kisses from
You Know Who

Twelfth Night

Darling Seb,

It's awful. I'm madly, desperately in love with Orsino, but, of course, he still thinks I'm *male*, and he's still obsessed with Olivia, and she seems to have got it really badly for me, because she sent me a ring the other day!! Can you believe it? And as for you, where on earth are you? I *know* you're not dead, I feel it in my bones, so I'm sending this to the port again.

Vi

Dear Buffy,

Just dropping you a line to tell you of a spiffing wheeze, a corking good joke. I'm staying at a bally great country house, with a frightfully good egg called Toby Belch. The place belongs to his niece, Olivia, and she's got this dreadful snooty butler, chap called Malvolio, who keeps trying to bust up our late night boozing sessions.

So what did old Toby and one of the maids do but send him a letter pretending to be from Toby's niece, saying how much she fancied him. The letter said – can you beat it? – he was to put on some *yellow leggings*, of all things, as a signal to her. So next morning at breakfast the chap turns up looking like a deranged pop star, all drooling with love for Her Ladyship. Never seen anything so funny in my life. Her Ladyship didn't take it too kindly, though. She had him packed off to the loony bin! Pretty good fun, eh, what?

Bung ho, old thing,
Andy A

FROM SIR TOBY BELCH TO SIR ANDREW AGUECHEEK

Listen, old bean, you ought to do something about that lad with the squeaky voice who keeps coming to see Olivia with messages from Orsino. If I'm not much mistaken, she's taken a shine to him – the lad, I mean. Unless you get him out of the way, there's not much chance of your marrying her yourself. Challenge him to a duel, old boy. A brilliant swordsman like you should be able to put him out of action in a trice.

T

FROM SIR TOBY BELCH TO MARIA

Do pop down to the rose garden after lunch. Would you believe it, I've egged that nincompoop Andy into challenging the lad from Orsino's to a duel! Of course, Andy doesn't know one end of a sword from the other, but I've told the lad he's the best duellist in Europe, so the lad's all of a quiver! And I've persuaded Andy that the lad got his fencing colours at university, whereas the truth is he's obviously never handled a weapon in his life. Should be a hoot! Come and watch it in the rose garden at 2.30 p.m.

T

Shakespeare Without the Boring Bits

Hi, Jim!

You know I got this summer job as resident comic in this big country house? Well, it's all been quite a scream. First of all, we persuaded the butler that the owner of the place, Lady Olivia, was in love with him, and he made such an ass of himself that they thought he was a nutter and packed him off. Then we had the most extraordinary goings on, like something out of a TV sitcom – you wouldn't believe it could happen in real life.

A young guy, who'd been working for a duke living down the road, kept turning up every day with love-letters from the duke to Lady Olivia. Well, she wasn't having any of it, but she fell for the messenger lad, who called himself Cesario. Meanwhile an upper-class twit called Sir Andrew Aguecheek has been staying here, and Olivia's uncle, an old boozer called Belch, put *him* up to the idea of marrying Olivia. And when Belch notices that Olivia fancies Cesario, he tells Aguecheek to challenge Cesario to a duel!

Tangled up, ain't it? But there's more to come. Neither Aguecheek nor Cesario really wants to fight, and they're both waving rapiers at each other nervously when along from the port comes a sailor, and he starts calling Cesario 'Sebastian', and claims he's just saved Sebastian's life.

The next thing we know, Olivia turns up and says she's just got married to Cesario. Well, Cesario doesn't know a thing about it – and he suddenly reveals that he isn't a lad at all. He's a girl, called Viola. Can you beat it?

At which point *another* Cesario turns up, absolutely the spitting image of the first one. Turns out it's Viola's twin, Sebastian. It was his life the sailor had saved.

Anyway, it all ends happily. It was Sebastian that Olivia had married, and when Orsino sees that 'Cesario' is really a very dishy girl, he says he'll marry *her*. So everyone's happy – except the butler!

Cheers,
Feste

FROM MALVOLIO TO EVERYONE AT LADY OLIVIA'S

I'll be REVENGED on the whole PACK of you!!!

A Midsummer Night's Dream

SUNG BY BOTTOM, IN A PUB

BOTTOM:

Now, someone buy me another drink,
And I'll tell you a tale that'll make you think,
Of how, though I am fat and hairy,
I was chatted up by a bloomin' fairy.

ALL:

Good old Bottom, buy him a half,
He may be a buttock but he makes us laugh.

A Midsummer Night's Dream

BOTTOM:
It was for the royal wedding day
That our drama club rehearsed a play,
A bit of a show for the Duke and his bride,
Out of doors if fine, if it rained, inside.
Peter Quince, who works on a building site,
Was our producer, and we met one night
To work out who was going to play what.
Now as an actor I'm pretty hot,
I can throw my voice like a kiddie's Frisbee.
Well, we were doing *Pyramus and Thisby*.
The story's a bit like *Romeo and Juliet*,
About a girl who hasn't left school yet.
The bloke who loves her thinks she's dead,
So he goes and chops off his bloomin' head.
We didn't argue who would star:
I was the one whose career would go far.
It's true that I work in a clothing factory,
But just look at me – you can *see* I'm actory.
They cast me as Pyramus (romantic lead),
But after that it was hard to proceed.
We needed a gorgeous, pouting co-star –
Not some old bat with a face like a toaster.
And though we'd been meeting since September,
We hadn't a single female member.

So we had to settle for Frankie Flute,
A chap with a face like a worn-out boot.
Frank's got a bit of a squeaky voice,
But you wouldn't call him the perfect choice
To play a creature that stirs up lust.
We'd have to put him in a padded bust.
Pete sent out a rehearsal call,
But we couldn't afford to hire a hall,
So to get us right into the mood
We all set off to a deep dark wood.

Now, it was a night of balmy weather.
As we were getting our scripts together
Under a tree, on a grassy slope,
There comes a pair wanting to elope.
Her name was Hermia, his Lysander;
They fancied each other like a goose and gander,
But her dad was playing the heavy father;
Instead of Lysander, he said he'd rather
She married Demetrius. He put it stronger:
She mustn't see Lysander for a moment longer.
So here they come, and a moment later
Follows Demetrius like a mad dictator.
He fancies Hermia, sweet as honey,
Not for her looks – but for her old man's money.

A Midsummer Night's Dream

And just to complete this mad quartet,
Comes someone I haven't mentioned yet:
A kid called Helena, sweet and gentle,
But Demetrius is driving her mental.
She loves him, but *his* great big pash
Is all for Hermia – or Hermia's cash.

Now tell me, do you believe in fairies?
Don't you look at me like deaf canaries!
I'd never seen a fairy – well, what would you
    think? –
Least, not till I'd had a lot to drink.
That evening I was completely sober,
Hadn't been pissed since last October,
But it's the truth that I'm recalling:
That wood with fairies was simply crawling.
Some of *them* were drunk, but one real sober one
Was the big boss fairy, name of Oberon.
With his missis he was having a quarrel;
Her behaviour had certainly been immoral
(Fairies don't keep rules, and the habit's
    catching).
She'd been doing a bit of cradle-snatching,
Had Titania, she'd pinched a nipper
With a face as smooth as a new-cooked kipper,

Brought him back to be her servant.
But Oberon, he was real observant,
Fancied the lad for his own staff too,
And when she said 'no', he sure was blue.
Ranted and raged and shouted his head off,
But as for Titania, she just sped off,
Said 'No go', and left him roarin',
Kicked so hard that he staved the door in.
Called his henchman, a boy named Puck,
Who could fly with the speed of a ten-ton truck,
Told him to fetch a certain potion
That smelt as sweet as a bathtime lotion,
Smear it on Titania's eyes,
So she'd get a big surprise,
Fall for the first thing she saw when she'd wake
   up,
Before she had time to do her make up.
This was Oberon's revenge,
So Puck fetched the stuff (from near Stone-
   henge)
And Oberon smeared it on Titania's lids,
And then Puck smeared it on the kids,
The lovers wandering in the wood –
So it stirred 'em up like a Christmas pud.
If you want to know what happened, why,

Get me a pint, 'cos my throat's real dry.
(*They buy him another drink.*)

ALL:
Good old Bottom, good old rump,
You may be a sit-upon, but you're no chump.

BOTTOM:
The lovers get in a right old tangle –
Puck's mixed them up from every angle –
But who falls for who I can't rightly say.
If you want to find out, read Shakespeare's play!
We've reached the important bit, you see,
The bit where the hero – yes! – is *me*.
For we were having our rehearsing,
And I was speechifying and versing,
And getting a laugh with every joke.
At the end of my scene I went for a smoke,
And at that moment, thanks to luck,
Up comes nimble Master Puck.
He needs a hunk to make Titania swoon,
And he sees me by the light of the moon.
'There's my man!' he sings, right *on* key,
'But I'm s'posed to make Titania seem a *don*key.
'She mustn't fall for looks, like any lass –

'I'll have to turn this fellow into an ass.'
And so – and I am not committing perjury –
He did a little fairy plastic surgery,
Lengthening my ears just a teensy bit,
Widening each nostril's delicate slit,
Until (and please don't split your sides)
I'd have looked at home giving donkey rides.

Titania wakens, and she is not
Fooled by these changes, not one jot.
She opens her eyes, and she sees *me*,
And falls in love, as deep as can be.
She notes where every handsome curve is,
Then presses the bell to call room service.
Up come fairies with wine and glasses,
And bags of hay (as served to asses).
Gallons of champers, if we felt boozy,
And a bubble bath in a hot Jacuzzi.
Oh dear, that night was too soon over,
And when I woke I had a foul hangover.
They'd given me back my usual face,
While of Ms Titania there wasn't a trace.
Some bloke told me, later on,
She'd made it up with Oberon.
And those poor kids whom Puck had muddled,

A Midsummer Night's Dream

He sorted out, and they all cuddled!

Well, friends, after all that strange reversal
I was nearly late for the dress rehearsal.
But I made it – the curtain went up on time,
And we showed the Duke and Duchess our
  pantomime.
We made 'em laugh, we made 'em cry,
They gave us ten curtain calls by and by.
So, friends, it was really the night of my life,
But I can't help remembering the Fairy King's
  wife,
Smiling all over her lovely chops,
Crooning: 'Darling Bottom, you're just the tops!'

The Merchant of Venice

TOLD BY LANCELOT GOBBO,
SHYLOCK'S SERVANT

To Messrs Montague & Capulet
Bankers
Verona

Gentlemen,

I beg to enquire whether there is any chance of obtaining employment in your office. For the past five years I have held a responsible position in the distinguished Venetian merchant banking house of Shylock & Shylock, but circumstances now make it necessary for me to seek a new post.

The bank's chairman, Mr Shylock, has recently undergone a business misfortune which has obliged him to cease trading, under somewhat distressing circumstances. (Please pardon the smudge in the above sentence. It occurred when the bailiffs carelessly knocked over my ink bottle while throwing me out into the street, along with Mr Shylock's few remaining items of property.)

Our chairman's judgement of credit-worthiness in the bank's clients was always faultless, and no one in the Venetian business world would have predicted that such a pillar of the financial community as Mr Antonio would default on the repayment of the substantial loan he had from us (this was on account of several cargo ships of his ownership all sinking at once).

The loss of the sum advanced to Mr Antonio would have been a small matter for our firm, had not our chairman agreed somewhat unusual terms with the client. This occasioned because the client, Mr Antonio, was in the deplorable habit of lending money to other members of the business community without charging interest, a practice which you will agree strikes at the heart of the financial world, especially at banking houses such as ourselves, which owe their very existence to realistic interest rates.

For his part, Mr Antonio claimed to deplore professional 'money-lending' (a crude term he chose to use for merchant banking), and only approached us for a loan because his cash-flow was temporarily impeded by business activities, and he wished to give financial assistance to a young friend, a Mr Bassanio. This gentleman needed the wherewithal to kit himself out for travelling to a country mansion, Belmont, there to woo, in some style, the wealthy young lady of the house, a Miss Portia.

It was Miss Portia's habit to set a kind of party game for the young gentlemen who fancied her. She would put out three boxes, one made of gold, one of silver and one of lead, and tell them to guess which one contained her portrait. She believed that anyone who went for the gold or the silver must be after her money. Mr Bassanio sensibly chose the lead box, and acquired the lady. (This has nothing to do with my job application, gentlemen, and I apologize for straying from the matter in hand.) Meanwhile, Mr Antonio was in the unfortunate situation of realizing that he could not repay the loan, on account of his ships having sunk to the bottom of the sea.

This, it must be admitted, was exactly what our chairman had hoped would happen, as it allowed him to put into effect Clause 9(b), paragraph (3) of the loan agreement he had drawn up with Mr Antonio. This stated that, should the loan not be repaid, our chairman was entitled to cut off a piece of Mr Antonio's flesh, weighing 453.59 grams, or to use the old system of weights, one pound, this to be removed from any part of the client's body at our chairman's discretion.

This unusual agreement naturally caused something of a stir in the business community, especially when it became known that the due date of repayment had passed without our chairman receiving Mr Antonio's cheque. It was announced that legal proceedings were to be instituted at once by our chairman, so as to obtain the aforesaid 453.59 grams of Mr Antonio's flesh.

Miss Portia (or Mrs Bassanio as she had now

become) took a keen interest in the financial world, being a lady of not inconsiderable means, and when she heard of these developments she and her personal assistant laid plans for (if you will pardon the expression) saving Mr Antonio's bacon, or at least 453.59 grams of it, seeing as how his predicament had arisen on account of his generosity to her husband.

She and the PA – a lady named Miss Nerissa, whom, I omitted to mention, had simultaneously become married to Mr Bassanio's companion, Mr Gratiano – set off for Venice without informing their husbands, and there managed to kit themselves out in lawyers' wigs and gowns, making out that they were, respectively, a distinguished barrister from Padua by the name of Mr Bellario, and his clerk. They then had themselves engaged as lawyers by Mr Antonio.

The following is a transcript of the court proceedings:

JUDGE:
Now, er, Mr Shylock, this is all a jolly good joke, threatening to chop off a chap's whatsit – I imagine that's what you've got in mind, old chap?

MR SHYLOCK:
Actually, no. His heart was the bit I'd got my eye on.
[commotion in court]

JUDGE:
Well, a joke's a joke, but his friends have all rallied round and offered you twice the money, so why don't you take it and call the whole thing off?

MR SHYLOCK:
Sorry, my lord, but a contract is a contract.
[Looks around]
Has somebody sharpened that knife for me?
[more commotion]

MR ANTONIO [undoing his shirt]:
It's a waste of time arguing. I know what these merchant bankers are. Let's get on with it.
[still more commotion]

MR BELLARIO [counsel for Mr Antonio, getting to his feet]:
If my client would allow me to conduct his case,

I would venture to ask Mr Shylock if he might consider being merciful to my client?

MR SHYLOCK:
No.

MR BELLARIO:
I see. In that case, my client might as well get on with undoing the other buttons.
[even more commotion, and cries of 'Antonio, get yourself a better lawyer!']

MR SHYLOCK [delighted]:
Excellent class of lawyer they're turning out from law school these days.

MR BELLARIO:
Thank you. And as you will have noticed, I have here a very accurate weighing machine, to check that it's 453.59 grams you've cut off my client.

MR SHYLOCK:
Fine, fine. [Someone hands him the knife, and he tests it]
Just the job. Here we go then.

MR BELLARIO:
Exactly 453.59 grams, mind you. That's what's written in the contract.

MR SHYLOCK [slightly uneasily]:
Ah yes. Exactly 453 grams.

MR BELLARIO:
No, exactly 453.59. Not 0.60, or for that matter 0.58.

MR SHYLOCK [sweating slightly]:
Well, I don't know I can get it quite as precisely as that. I mean, I'm not one of those microsurgeons. Can I put a bit back if I take too much?

MR BELLARIO:
Not according to the contract.

MR SHYLOCK [turning rather pale]:
Ah, I see.

MR BELLARIO:
Well, it was you who drew up the contract, wasn't it? And, of course, no blood.

MR SHYLOCK [loosening his collar]:
I beg your pardon?

MR BELLARIO:
Not a drop of my client's blood may be shed.
Not one single drop.

MR SHYLOCK:
That is ridiculous. It says in the contract that
I can cut this bit off him. How on earth
am I supposed to do that without shedding
blood?

MR BELLARIO:
My dear Mr Shylock, you should have thought
of that when you drew up the contract.
[laughter in court]

MR ANTONIO [beaming]:
Excellent class of lawyer they're turning out
from law school these days.

MR SHYLOCK:
Er, my lord, I think I'll take the money after
all.

MR BELLARIO:
Sorry, Mr Shylock, but a contract is a contract.
[More laughter]
Isn't that true, my lord?

JUDGE [waking up]:
Whatever you say, Mr Bellario. I must confess
this whole case is rather beyond me.

MR BELLARIO:
But not beyond me, my lord. My client has
already refused the offer of the money owed
him, with the words 'a contract is a contract'.
The contract obliges him to detach 453.58 –

EVERYONE IN COURT:
453.59.

MR BELLARIO:
So sorry. [Laughter] To detach 453.59 grams of
my client's flesh, but *precisely* that amount, and
without spilling even one milligram of blood. So,
get on with it, Mr Shylock.

MR SHYLOCK [gathering his papers and putting
away the knife]:
My lord must be aware that counsel for Mr

Antonio is asking the impossible. If Mr Antonio will repay me the sum I lent him, without interest, I shall be content to drop the matter. [cheers in court]

MR BELLARIO:
But I will not. By declaring his intention to cut this piece from the region of my client's heart, Mr Shylock has, in effect, announced his intention of killing him. Do you agree, my lord?

JUDGE [waking up again]:
Er, well, I suppose so, yes.

MR BELLARIO:
And you know the penalty for that, my lord, under Venetian law?

JUDGE:
Well, er, I can't call it to mind right now.

MR BELLARIO:
The penalty, my lord, is that anyone the courts find guilty of plotting to kill someone must give up half of his wealth to his intended victim ...

MR SHYLOCK:
Strewth! Well, at least it's only half.

MR BELLARIO:
. . . and half to the government.

MR SHYLOCK [gulping]:
Do you mind if I sit down? Not feeling very well.

MR ANTONIO:
I don't want half his goods; I'll settle for a quarter, and when I die I'll leave it to the chap who recently eloped with his daughter.
[Antonio is carried shoulder high out of the court, to shouts of 'For he's a jolly good fellow'. Mr Shylock is smuggled through the crowd in a blanket]

When it was discovered that 'Mr Bellario' was in fact a lady completely without legal qualifications, there was some call for the case to come to court again, but by that time our chairman had slipped away from Venice with a number of other clients' funds. Despite repeated reports of sightings in the newspapers, the international police have not been able to trace him.

I am consequently out of a job, and am thinking of moving to Verona, where I gather the pace of life in the business world is somewhat quieter. I am sure, gentlemen, that rumours which have reached Venice, about the heads of your firm, Mr Montague and Mr Capulet, falling out with each other, are considerably exaggerated.

I look forward to your prompt reply.

Yours sincerely,

L. Gobbo (Mr)

Macbeth

TOLD BY MACBETH

Call me Mac.

It was the kind of day when you can do your washing without taking your clothes off. That's to say, damp. Banquo and I were damp all right. And not just from the rain. We'd been beating the hell out of a bunch of rebels and Norwegians. And I'm not talking about tennis.

Scotland's a big place, and we had most of it to cross to get home. A lot of the scenery looks as though someone backstage is having a joke, and this bit was no exception. They called it a blasted heath. It looked as if whoever drew it had been trying to rub it out ever since. Kind of weird.

But not as weird as the three dames we ran into. I mean, I've seen all kinds of broads, but this trio made me realize I had to redefine the species. If Helen of Troy had a face that launched a thousand ships, this lot would have sent any fleet into a mudbank.

'Hail!' yelled out the youngest of them, and she wouldn't see ninety-five again. I looked up into the sky. Well, I thought she was talking about the weather!

'All hail, Macbeth!' screamed the second, who'd passed her sell-by date a couple of centuries ago. 'Hail, Thane of Cawdor.'

'You got the wrong guy, ladies,' I told them. But they hadn't finished their little production number.

'All hail, Macbeth, who'll be king one day!' screamed the third, who made the other two look like winners in a beautiful baby contest.

Now, I'm the last guy to mind a compliment from an older woman, but this was ridiculous. No one gets to be king unless he's got royal blood in his veins. Or unless he drains a bucketful of the stuff out of its rightful owners.

'What about me, ladies?' snaps out Banquo. 'Don't I get nothing?'

'No throne for you, big boy,' says the third crone, the one who looks like she's just taking five minutes off from being dead. 'But your kids'll be sitting on it all right.'

'Ladies, talk sense,' I told them, but suddenly they were nowhere to be seen. I was just wondering whether it was something I ate, when up come a couple of guys with a message from the king. They told me he liked the way I'd recycled those rebels into crow food. In fact, he liked it so much he was going to make me Thane of Cawdor.

I called my wife, told her the news. If that close-harmony trio had got it right about me being Thane of Cawdor, chances were the king bit might be on the line too. I told her that.

She liked it. And when I got home she had news for me. The king was checking in for the night. Into our guest bedroom. 'See to it that he doesn't get any breakfast,' my wife told me. And it wasn't his diet she had in mind.

Round about the cocktail hour, the king steps on to our front porch. 'I like the view here, folks,' he tells everyone. Enjoy it, king. It's the last you're ever gonna see.

I wasn't feeling so good about what I had to do. As kings go, he was a good one. And now he'd really gotta go. 'I ain't doin' it,' I told my wife.

She had a few things to say to me about that. Like how she was gonna give me a new name. Coward was the name she had in mind. And a lot more like that. 'OK,' I told her, 'I'm doin' it.'

What a broad. And she had a plan. The king had the usual crowd with him, bodyguards, hair-dressers, you know the stuff. She served them up a nightcap with a kick like the acceleration of a getaway car. Besides the liquor, there was a certain little white powder in it. Those guys weren't gonna wake till morning, not if you'd tickled the soles of their feet with a dentist's drill.

By this time, I was strung up to such a pitch I was seeing daggers before my eyes. And they weren't pointing to the exit doors.

A few minutes later, there was a lot of blood about the place. The king's blood. And most of it was all over me.

I could see my wife didn't think the colour red suited me. Nor was she too keen that I was carrying a handful of daggers. 'Get back in there,' she hissed, 'and make it look as if his servants did it.'

'Lady,' I said, 'I'm not going back in there.' Quite apart from the king looking like someone had been trying to turn him into several orders of steak tartare, I'd been hearing this voice, saying I wouldn't be sleeping no more. Not for the rest of my born days. Which wasn't exactly the king's problem. Just then, someone knocked at our front door. I wished they could have woken the king. But he'd dropped off into the big sleep.

The guy beating a drum-break on the door was a fella named Macduff. He had an appointment with the king. An early one. He was a spot late for it, though. He went into the king's bedroom and came out looking as if he'd just bet twelve million dollars on a horse. And lost.

'He's dead,' he snapped out.

'You don't say?' I said, acting as hard as if I were in line for an Academy Award.

Just at that moment, the king's sons, who were staying at our place with the rest of the crowd, wandered along to see what had happened. When they realized daddy wouldn't be tucking them up at night no more, they took one look at me, packed their bags, and got out of the place with the speed of an express elevator.

A couple of days later, I was sitting around in my crown, thinking how swell it was to be king, when I recalled what those geriatric chorus-girls had told Banquo about his descendants becoming king after me. That didn't sound so good. So I called up a couple of guys I knew.

Swell guys, these. So tough they made Al Capone look like Minnie Mouse. 'Hi, fellas,' I greeted them. 'I got a guy called Banquo and his kid son coming over here for a meal. See he gets a knuckle sandwich instead.'

'Just that, boss?' they grunted.

'Not just that. I'd like some local undertaker to be making enough dough today to take his wife and kiddies to the seaside.' I'm such a soft-hearted individual.

'We get you, boss,' they said. And sure enough, a couple of hours later, Banquo was being measured for a wooden overcoat. But not his kid, who'd run off when the fat hit the fire.

Just because Banquo was dead, it didn't mean we shouldn't lay a place for him at table. A lot of the smart set were coming to dinner, and it doesn't do to let on you've just introduced one of your guests to the grim reaper. So there was Banquo's knife and fork.

And jeez, there was Banquo, looking like he'd just been through somebody's office shredder. And he was the colour of the day-before-yesterday's milk (apart from the blood, which was all over him, and was the usual red). 'Get the hell out of here!' I snapped at him. 'Don't you know you're dead?'

Seems he agreed with me, because he just vanished, the way those sweet old ladies had done. Talking of them, I reckoned it was time I paid them another visit.

As blasted heaths go, this one was looking more blasted than ever. And my lady friends were brewing up a bit of lunch. You know the sort of menu, eye of newt, tongue of dog, leg of lizard. The kind of things you can get at any witches' lunch-counter.

'How's the future looking?' I asked them. So they told me. Or rather, they laid on a show.

You've heard of special guest appearances? Well, these were special ghost appearances. And I just sat there listening, and freaked out. A case of spook when you're spooken to.

'Beware Macduff!' snapped out the first ghost, but the second one said I didn't need to fuss myself about any guy who'd been born of a woman. Which I reckoned meant I had nothing to fear from one hundred per cent of the population.

Then up comes another of these freaks, this time to tell me I wouldn't bite the dust till Birnam Wood marched up Dunsinane Hill. Suited me, since most woods I know like to stay put. But what about Banquo's descendants, I asked them. Was there any truth in the nasty little rumour that they, and not my kids, if I had any, would become king after me?

For an answer, who should pop up but Banquo again, showing me his family photo album. And sure enough, all the kids were wearing crowns.

That was all I needed to make my day. And no sooner was I back home than some guy tells me Macduff has fled to England, and is getting a lot of guys together to pay a visit to me. Not the friendliest of visits.

Well, two can play at that game. He'd made a little mistake, had Macduff. He'd left his family behind. So I got those guys who'd done such a nice job on Banquo to pay a call on the Macduffs. Next day, there weren't no Macduffs left to call on.

Things were starting to get hot for me. You've heard of rats leaving a sinking ship? Well, let's just say the vermin count at my place was going down by the hour.

Then there was my wife. She'd taken to washing her hands. Approximately ninety-seven times an hour! To get the blood off, she said, though there wasn't any blood that I could see.

Yes, the poor dame was losing her mind. And I thought my own had decided to say goodbye to me when I looked out of the window and saw a lot of trees on the march. Sure enough, it was Birnam Wood, come to see how things were doing on Dunsinane Hill.

Now, the habits of trees don't greatly concern me, but after a while it struck me that all this travelling timber was just a load of camouflage. I mean, real trees don't carry swords.

Yeah, they'd come to get me, and just as my

wife had decided it was time she tried out her grave for size. I was rattled, I admit, but if it was curtains for me, I was gonna take a hell of a lot of guys with me.

Sure enough, in a few minutes, my sword had managed to investigate quite a few sets of guts. Then who should come up for a personal encounter but Macduff. 'Save your strength,' I told him. 'No one who was born of a woman can harm me. Which just about rules out the whole of homo sapiens.'

'Sorry to disappoint you,' smirks Macduff. 'Ever heard of a caesarean? My ma was gonna have a difficult labour, so they cut me out. Geddit?'

I got it, all right. And I got his sword too. Right where it hurts most.

If I ever meet those three weird sisters in the next world, I've got a bone to pick with them.

The Taming of the Shrew

Dear Women's Refuge,

I am writing to ask if you have a place for me. Most women want to go and live in Refuges to get away from violent husbands. I want to get away from my violent sister, Kate.

She has been tormenting me since we were tiny. She bites, kicks, scratches and hits me. She even ties a rope to my hands, and drags me round the house. This is the sort of thing that lots of sisters do to each other when they are children, but Kate is twenty-seven and I am twenty-two. It has got to stop.

Lots of men want to marry me, and take me away from Kate, but my father says he won't let anyone marry me till Kate has found a husband. Of course, I am old enough to get married without his consent, and I am jolly good-looking, but I'm afraid none of the men who fancy me will want to marry me if my father doesn't give them a lot of money as a marriage settlement.

So I am stuck. And covered with scratches and bruises.

Help, she is coming for me now, I can hear her roaring up the stairs. I must hide this letter. She will murder me if she sees it.

Yours in terror,
Bianca Minola

Dear Women's Refuge,

It's all right, I managed to hide the letter, and I escaped with only a couple more scratches. But it isn't just physical violence. She's got a tongue as sharp as a chain-saw. She just insults everyone, men and women alike, so, of course, no one wants to marry her.

What on earth am I going to do?

Yours in increasing desperation,
Bianca Minola

Dear Women's Refuge,

I am writing to ask if you can find a place for me to come and live in the Refuge. I know it's meant for people escaping from horrible husbands, but I want to get away from my horrible sister, Bianca.

She has been horrible to me ever since we were both young, and what's worse, so has my father. It's been awful for me, ever since she was born, because she's pretty and I'm not. She's got the sort of baby-doll looks that all men seem to go for, including fathers. So, all through our childhood, everything I did was wrong if Bianca didn't like it.

I'm five years older than her, I've got a right

to a life of my own, but my father has never let me have one. He's given Bianca all the lovely clothes she's ever asked for, and I have to dress in her hand-me-downs – *hers*, even though she's my younger sister – because he says I look a fright, and good clothes would be wasted on me.

Well, of course I look a fright, because I spend half my day crying in misery. And then Bianca comes and laughs at me for being a cry-baby, and sometimes I lose my temper and hit her, and then you should hear the terrible fuss that father makes. He talks about having me locked up, and all sorts of horrible things.

All I want to do is leave home. But I've got nowhere to go. Bianca has all sorts of ghastly men hanging round her, longing to marry her – though I reckon that's as much because they want to get their hands on father's money, as for her looks. She can get married for all I care. Good riddance to her.

But the trouble is, father won't let anyone marry her till he's got a husband for me. As if I wanted a husband! I can't stand men – not if they're like father, or the men who want to marry Bianca. And those are the only men I know.

So, please can I come and live at the Refuge? I can't pay you any money, because father won't let me have any, but I'm very good at cleaning floors and washing up. And I'm big and strong, and will work all the hours you want me to.

Yours hopefully,
Kate Minola

Dear Women's Refuge,

I don't think I'm going to need to come and live in the Refuge after all. The most extraordinary thing has happened. Someone has turned up who says he wants to marry my sister Kate.

His name is Petruchio, he's just inherited a country house and some money, because his father has died, and he says he's travelling the world to find a wife, preferably a rich one. He's quite open about wanting more money. And when he heard about Kate, he said he'd marry her, just like that.

Yes, he'd heard everything about her – how she tormented me night and day, and didn't have a polite word in her head. Petruchio said he didn't care tuppence. He liked a woman with some spirit. And he told father he'd marry her in a couple of days' time.

Father was completely gobsmacked about this, of course. Absolutely delighted, but a bit worried that he ought to get Kate's agreement to it. As if it mattered what *she* thought, after the way she's behaved to me and everyone!

So he left Petruchio in the room, and sent Kate downstairs to meet him. And no one knows what they said to each other, but in a few minutes Kate had come out of the room, giggling, and said she was going to order her wedding dress right away.

Meanwhile, I've chosen my own husband, a frightfully dishy creature called Lucentio, who says he's got pots of money. He's been pretending to be a poor scholar, and he got a job as my tutor, so he could chat me up! Would you believe it! He's going to explain everything to my father, and get his agreement, so it'll all be wonderful. Lucentio isn't at all mad like Petruchio. He's frightfully sensible. So I can't wait to get married to him.

Yours excitedly,
Bianca Minola

Dear Women's Refuge,

I'm writing to you because I'm a bit embarrassed about my last letter, and I thought you ought to know that things have suddenly come right. I've found a husband!!!

I know I said I didn't like men, but this one is different. He's big and noisy and funny, and doesn't take no for an answer, from *anyone*, not even me. He makes me laugh, and no one's ever done that before.

Actually, he tricked me into agreeing to marry him. He and my father had it all sewn up between them before *I* was ever asked – typical men! – and when my father sent me to meet him, I told Petruchio I'd rather see him hanged than marry him. But he just laughed, and grabbed hold of me and kissed me, and then my father came back into the room, and Petruchio said everything was settled. I was furious, and I started hitting out at him, the way I do with my sister when I lose my temper, because I could tell that words wouldn't have any effect. My father looked worried. But Petruchio just laughed that mad laugh of his, and said, 'You see, we've agreed that in front of other people she'll pretend she's still a bad-tempered bitch. It's only when we're alone together that she really lets on that she's passionately in love with me!'

Well, I just couldn't help admiring his quick wit, and I started laughing, and in next to no time I was in the dress shop, being measured for my wedding things!

I just thought you'd like to know how the story ended. I think he's going to be a great husband.

> Yours in blissful anticipation,
> *Kate Minola*

Dear Women's Refuge,

I was wrong. He's not going to be a great husband. He's terrible, and if I had the strength, I would run away tonight. I'll make it to the Refuge soon, I really will. Please keep a bed for me.

For a start, he turned up at our wedding hours late, and looking like a drunken tramp, in dreadful old clothes. And he dragged me into church, hit the clergyman with a prayer book, and then, when the service was over, wouldn't let me stay for the reception. We had to ride off straight away to his country house.

Country house! It was more like a shed!!! Full of draughts, and in the middle of a muddy farm-yard, so that in no time at all I was absolutely filthy. I was cold and starving and exhausted, but when we sat down to supper, he wouldn't let me eat a thing. He kept sending the food back, saying it was burnt, or undercooked, or some-thing else was wrong with it. NOTHING was wrong with it. It was just him torturing me. And when I collapsed into bed, he wouldn't let me sleep. He kept fussing with the bedclothes and the curtains and everything in the room, saying it wasn't quite right. He pretended he was doing it because he wanted only the best of everything for me, but of course it was all to wear me down, to break my spirit.

This went on for days and days and days. And in the end I had no resistance left. He was making me say stupid things, like agreeing that the sun was really the moon. Well, I didn't care any longer. And now we're on the journey back to my father's house, and I still haven't eaten or slept for nearly a week. If I don't die of this, please, please take me in and let me escape from him.

Yours at the end of her tether,
Kate Minola

Dear Women's Refuge,

I was going to write you a letter asking you to help my sister Kate, because she was in such a dreadful state. But actually I'm the one who needs your help now.

Kate came back from her honeymoon looking terrible. I asked her if Petruchio had been beating her, but she said no. He'd done everything else, however, to give her a horrible time. Hadn't let her eat or sleep for days and days. She was just a broken wreck. Absolutely the sort of person who needed your help.

And then it happened. Father was very shocked by her appearance, but he decided to go ahead with the celebration dinner party that he'd planned for my wedding to Lucentio, which had just taken place. Well, we all ate and drank a lot (especially Kate, who was still starving), and then Kate and I went into the sitting-room to talk, leaving the men to finish their drinks. Well, after a few minutes someone came in with a message that Lucentio wanted me back in the dining-room. There was no explanation, and no 'please', so I sent a message back that I was busy. A few minutes later, the message came that Petruchio *ordered* Kate to go into the dining-room. I thought this was a dreadful cheek, and told her to say no, but she just got up and went. And a moment later she came back and told me to return to the dining-room with her. I didn't see why I should, and I told her so, but then she got that old look in her eye that she used to have when she was going to hit me, so I got up and went.

And when we arrived at the table, Petruchio cheered and clapped, and it turned out he'd won a big bet against Lucentio as to which of them could get their wives to come when they ordered them. Monstrous! But there was worse to come.

Petruchio said, 'Now, Kate, tell all of us what a woman's duty to her husband is.'

Kate just laughed and said, 'To obey him, that's all. It isn't very hard. Someone's got to make the decisions in the marriage and it might as well be the man. I can't see the point of all this fuss about women's rights.'

All the men cheered at this, including, I'm afraid, my own Lucentio. Well! Give me back the old Kate, who bit and fought and scratched, at least she stood up for herself. And if that's what marriage is about, Lucentio can keep it.

Could you put a hot water bottle in my bed, please?

Looking forward to seeing you tonight,
Bianca Minola

Henry the Fifth

TOLD BY THE CHORUS*

SHAKES:

This is Bill Shakes reporting for *News at Ten* from outside the royal palace in London.

England has a new king, Henry the Fifth, and everyone's saying that he is a reformed character. Remember all those scandals in the tabloids about his behaviour when he was Prince of Wales? Drinking in shady pubs with members of the

---

* The Chorus in *Henry the Fifth* is an actor who reports and comments on the action, much like a TV news reporter today.

criminal classes, and playing disgraceful practical jokes with Sir John Falstaff, the fattest aristocrat in England? Well, those days are past, say sources close to the king. Meet him now, and he talks like an archbishop, a politician or a general. He's a force to be reckoned with.

But in France, they haven't caught up with this change. They've heard that Henry's got his eye on the French throne – he wants to take an English army across the Channel, and show them who's the top dog. This plan for an away match isn't just a piece of macho muscle-baring, because Henry really has a legitimate claim to be king of France.

The French aren't taking him seriously yet, and today they've been doing their best to insult him. With me is the king's uncle, the Duke of Exeter. Your Grace, can you tell me what happened?

DUKE OF EXETER:
Well, a couple of French diplomat chappies came to see us, with a parcel addressed to the king. They said it was 'treasure', something that suited the king's age and character.

SHAKES:
And when you opened it, what did you find?

DUKE OF EXETER:
Tennis balls.

SHAKES:
And what was the king's reaction?

DUKE OF EXETER:
I expect you can imagine. The British government has sent a message to the French government saying that, in return for these tennis balls, they're going to get a consignment of cannon balls. Ha, ha, ha!

SHAKES:
So it looks like war?

DUKE OF EXETER:
It certainly does.

SHAKES:
And with that, back to the studio.

*

NEWSREADER:

And the main headline tonight: British intelligence agents have managed to uncover and foil an assassination plot on the king. Over to our reporter Bill Shakes, who's in Southampton.

SHAKES:

Yes, here in Southampton, there's a sense of shock and relief at what's happened. The entire British army had just assembled here, ready for embarkation to France, when it was revealed that three top military officials, the Earl of Cambridge, Lord Scroop and Sir Thomas Grey, had been discovered in the act of accepting a bribe from the French government, to kill King Henry before he had a chance to set off for France. The British government has taken immediate action, and sources close to ministers believe that death-sentences on these three will be carried out at once. In fact, the three prisoners are just being brought along the quayside now, under armed guard, with ropes round their necks, so I think we can guess what that means. Let me see if I can get a word with one of them ... Lord Scroop, what have you got to say about the charge of treason, and the death sentence?

LORD SCROOP:
No comment.

SHAKES:
This is Bill Shakes, in Southampton, for *News at Ten*. No, wait, we've had a newsflash that the British government has just received an offer from Paris. Apparently the French king is offering his daughter Katherine as a wife for King Henry, plus an undisclosed sum of money and various areas of land in France, if Britain will call off its threat of aggression against the French. It's reported that the Princess Katherine is already learning English in preparation for her marriage. But we believe the offer has not been accepted by Britain. And with that, back to the studio.

*

NEWSREADER:
Day One of the French War. And *News at Ten*'s

correspondent is in the thick of the action. So, over to you, Bill Shakes, on the walls of Harfleur.

SHAKES:
Yes, and I hope you can hear me above the roaring of the guns. As you can see, the town of Harfleur is under intensive bombardment by the British forces, and they've managed to make a very considerable breach in its walls. Amazingly, King Henry himself is leading his troops into action – he's right there at the interface between British and French, risking his life and, if we zoom in, we may get a glimpse of him urging his men on.

KING HENRY [just audible above the noise of fighting]:
Back again, back into that gap! Come on, we're English. We're the toughest fighters in the world! And God's on our side – on the side of England, King Henry, and Saint George!

SHAKES:
And just listen to the reception he's getting from

his troops. They're cheering like a football crowd! And we've just heard that the military governor of Harfleur has decided to surrender. He was waiting for aid from the French army, but it simply hasn't come. So, on Day One, it's one nil to England! Good news as I hand you back to the studio.

*

NEWSREADER:

And on Day Two of the French War, our reporter Bill Shakes has disturbing news of trouble among the English army. Over to Bill Shakes in the Somme Valley.

SHAKES:

Yes, there's trouble in store for a number of English soldiers who haven't been obeying the rules of war. After yesterday's victory at Harfleur, British forces have been advancing steadily towards a confrontation with the whole French army. The mood is good, but considerable anxiety has been caused at military headquarters by news that British soldiers have been stealing and looting in some of the towns they've marched through. King Henry is reported to be taking the toughest possible line over this.

The bad behaviour is being put down to the fact that the British army is largely made up of recruits with very little military experience. Many of the troops come from Wales, Scotland and Ireland, and there have been complaints from the English soldiers that they spend more time chattering to each other than fighting. But the serious trouble actually involves a group of Londoners, men from the East End. A Private Bardolph was caught ransacking a church in a French village. He was at once court-martialled, and shot by order of the king himself. This must have been a particularly painful decision for the king to make, because Bardolph was one of the East-Enders he used to go drinking with, in the days of his association with Sir John Falstaff. We've also heard that Falstaff himself is dead – he died peacefully, of old age, in London, so he didn't live to hear the disgrace his old friend had fallen into.

Coming up soon will be the big military confrontation between British and French. I'll be reporting on the latest developments as news comes in.

*

BREAKFAST TV PRESENTER:
And now for a time-check — it's five a.m. It's still dark here in London, while over in France, our war correspondent Bill Shakes is rubbing the sleep from his eyes. Wakey, wakey, Bill!

SHAKES:
Well, actually, Brian, I've been up and about all night. Everyone here has, because the British and French armies have now come face to face — they're less than a mile apart, and there's no doubt that the big attack will come at daybreak. It's just a question of who moves first. And for the latest news, and a forecast of the day's events, I'm joined in our mobile studio by the leader of the British forces, the King of England himself. King Henry, what do you predict, a good day, or a bad one?

KING HENRY:
Well, Bill, I wouldn't be much of a general if I

said we were going to lose, but I won't pretend it'll be easy. I don't know whether you've seen the figures, but according to reliable sources there are about sixty thousand French troops – five times as many soldiers as we've got. And, of course, they're fresh too, whereas we're fairly weary after our triumph at Harfleur.

SHAKES:

So you don't reckon the British chances are too good?

KING HENRY:

I never said that, Bill. Look, we've got a wonderful team. I think we'll be tremendous.

SHAKES:

But you could do with at least another ten thousand?

KING HENRY:

No way. I don't want anybody else to share in the big win! Bill, I don't know if you've looked at your diary, but today is St Crispin's Day. I can promise you, that in years to come, there'll be people who fought in the British army today showing off their scars, and saying, 'I got that wound on St Crispin's Day, when we beat the French hollow!'

SHAKES:

And what about the rumour that you've been going round the ranks yourself, disguised as an ordinary soldier, having a chat to your men and finding out how they're feeling about the battle?

KING HENRY:

Yes, I've been on my feet all night, Bill, and I can tell you, we've got the loyalest, toughest soldiers in the world. Put your money on Britain, everyone!

SHAKES:

Well, Your Majesty, we'll let you get back to your operations HQ. Here on the French plains, near the town of Agincourt, the sun is starting to come up. The atmosphere is really tense. A cock is crowing, a clock is striking, and everyone's on tenterhooks, waiting for the first shot to be fired.

It won't be long. This is Bill Shakes at Agincourt, returning you to the studio in London.

*

ANNOUNCER:

We're interrupting this cartoon to bring you a newsflash. Over to our war correspondent Bill Shakes at Agincourt, France.

SHAKES:

And we've just heard that the French have conceded defeat, after a truly remarkable battle. Approximately ten thousand French troops were killed, including a large number of top generals, but the British losses were incredibly small – according to some reports, less than thirty men. There have already been top-level talks between the French and the British, and sources close to King Henry say he's accepted the French king's offer of his daughter Katherine and, more importantly, King Henry now becomes heir to the French throne. If he and the Princess Katherine have a son, he will become King of France. An excellent outcome for Britain, then, and a brisk finish to a war, which some predicted might last many months and escalate into a major European conflict. Later on, we'll be bringing you interviews with the British military leaders, including King Henry himself, and a team of experts will be discussing the implications of the British–French royal marriage and the future for both countries. But for now, I'll return you to the studio, and that whacky cartoon!

The Tempest

TOLD BY MIRANDA

We lived on an island. My father was a writer of children's books. At least, I suppose they were for children, because they were about the most wonderful, magical things.

I call them 'books', but I never saw any of them on the shelves. To me, they were simply amazing stories that he told me in the evenings, after he had hidden away all day, writing. They must have been meant for books, otherwise why would he have taken the trouble to write them? Surely not just so that he could entertain me in the evening, in front of the fire, and watch me laughing at the funny bits and crying at the sad parts.

He used to say that the stories weren't really made up by him. He said that all the hard work was done by two very curious people. One was a lively young lad, who would suddenly turn up when my father was least expecting him, and would do the most amazing things. My father might be struggling with a story, quite unable to get beyond the first couple of pages, and suddenly this lad would pour out all sorts of brilliant ideas, so that my father's only problem was to write fast enough to take them all down before he had forgotten them. He didn't know the lad's name at first, but after a while he started to call him 'Ariel', because it suggested somebody lighter than air, whizzing through the sky on a kind of magical errand to create a story for my father.

The other person who helped him wasn't some-one my father liked to talk about much. When he did mention him, he'd only say that this fellow turned up far too often, and the problem was usually how to get rid of him. Whereas Ariel was light and quick, this was a heavy, surly creature, fat and hairy, and not at all pleasant to look at. He smelt nasty, and he had all sorts of unpleasant habits. He was just as full of suggestions as Ariel, but they weren't pleasant ones. His ideas for stories usually involved killing people, or causing them great suffering, and other very unpleasant things best not mentioned.

My father had tried locking this creature, whom he called 'Caliban', out of his work-room altogether, but the curious thing was, he found he needed him, at least now and then. As wonderful as Ariel's ideas were, if there wasn't a bit of Caliban in a story (said my father), it didn't somehow ring true. It was apt to seem a bit too frothy and light and whimsical. Caliban, unpleasant as he was, brought things down to earth.

My father said that, as the years passed, he had gradually learned to get Ariel and Caliban under control, so that on the whole they came when he called them. Sometimes he even referred to them as his servants. But, by the time I was about fifteen, I began to sense that my father was getting weary of writing stories all the time. He said that Ariel kept demanding to be freed – the lad wanted to go off and write his own stories, or maybe give ideas to someone else. Maybe this was just my father's way of saying he, himself, was getting old and tired.

As for Caliban, my father said he was demanding to be given back the island, because it was really his. The island was the place where we lived. My father said it was perfectly true that Caliban had been there when we arrived, because Caliban is everywhere. I think he meant that, unless people make an effort, their lives will be just like Caliban's, unpleasant, uncomfortable and ugly. We have to work to make things better, not just stories, but life itself.

I've called the place where we lived an island, because that was how my father always spoke of it. I don't know whether it really was. It seemed to change all the time, depending on my father's stories. He was such a wonderful story-teller that, when he described an African forest with beasts roaring and trumpeting, I could see it in front of my eyes. And when his story was set in a big city, full of bustle and noise, I could not only see, but smell and hear it. I think that, had I wanted to, I could have got up and walked right into it. Our scenery seemed to change every day. So I don't know if we were really on an island.

I'm not even sure that my father *was* my father. When I asked, he used to say he was, but in a funny, jokey way which suggested that, after all, he might not be. Once, I told him that he must have been a king before he came to the island, because he was clever enough to have ruled a country. So he agreed with that, and said that once upon a time he had been King of Naples, until his wicked brother had thrown him out of the kingdom, and had set him adrift in a boat, so that he was carried right across the world before landing on the island. It was a very good story, but I'm not sure that it was more than a story.

I asked him whether I'd been cast adrift with him in that boat, so that together we had come across the sea to the island. He said yes, but he said it in the sort of way that meant he was story-telling. I don't know whether it was the truth. Once, he asked me, quite sharply, whether I remembered anything that had happened to me before I found myself on the island with him. I thought hard, but could only remember a vague picture of a woman looking after me when I was tiny. I suppose she was my mother. I asked my father about her, but she didn't seem to come into the story he was telling just then, and afterwards I forgot to ask him again.

So there was just him, and me, and the stories, until I was almost sixteen. And then one day, something terrible happened. I began to get bored.

Well, not exactly bored, but a feeling began to stir in me that there must be something else in the world besides my father's stories. I didn't say that to him; he would have been dreadfully upset. But I could tell from his eyes that he knew I wasn't listening with the same attention that I used to. And that was when the storm began.

It was just a story, of course, like everything else that happened on the island, but it was more real than any he had told me before. He described the crashing of the wind, the towering waves, the lightning that seemed to split the sky open, and the terrible explosion of the thunder. And he spoke in awful detail about the terror of the sailors on board the ship – there was a ship being tossed about in the storm, like a pebble in a child's hands – and how they shouted and screamed and ran for the lifeboats; but it was too late, because the ship had split in two, and was going down with all hands aboard.

I could see every bit of it in front of me, just as if it were really happening. And then he calmed the waves, and made the thunderstorm stop, and threw planks of wood and barrels about in the sea, so that everyone who had fallen into the water could grab something and float to safety. In a few moments, he had brought them all to dry land.

He said that Ariel had been doing all the work for him, but I could see that my father had thrown everything of himself into the story too, because he was looking quite exhausted.

'Chapter Two,' he went on, after taking a deep breath. He always divided his stories into chapters as he was telling them. 'When Ferdinand came to his senses, he found he was lying on a sunny beach, and he thought he heard a voice calling him.'

'Who's Ferdinand?' I asked. My father always hated to be interrupted, but this time he just looked a bit embarrassed.

'Didn't I tell you?' he muttered. 'Ferdinand was the handsome prince who had been shipwrecked along with the others. The son of the King of Naples.'

'Your son?' I asked, amazed. 'I didn't know I had a brother.'

'No, Miranda, not that. The son of the wicked fellow who displaced the rightful king.'

'Who displaced *you*, you mean?' I asked him.

He looked as if he had forgotten that he had once told me he was the dispossessed King of Naples. 'Ah, yes,' he said absent-mindedly. 'Well, perhaps we'll forget Ferdinand, and see what some of the other shipwrecked people were up to.'

'No, no,' I said excitedly. 'I want to hear about the handsome prince. We've never before had a story with a handsome prince in it.'

'Haven't we, my dear?' My father stroked his chin. He had a beard these days, and it was going very grey, like the rest of him.

'Was he as handsome as you?' I asked keenly. You see, my father was the only man I had ever seen, and when he described other men in his stories, I always imagined them as looking like him, if they were handsome.

My father sighed. 'Rather more so,' he said. 'You see, he was ... young.' And as he spoke, I could see Ferdinand.

Really see him, I mean. Like the storm,

Ferdinand was more real than any person he had ever described before in a story. He was walking up the beach towards us. And I gasped.

'Is he a god, like the ones in those Greek stories you told me?' I asked my father. 'I've never seen anything so beautiful.'

My father groaned quietly to himself. 'No, just an ordinary young man,' he said sadly. 'It had to happen one day.'

Ferdinand had stopped, and was staring at us. Well, at me. 'Are you a goddess?' he called out. 'Surely you can't be human?'

'Go on, speak to him,' hissed my father. 'Get it all over with.'

Slowly, I got to my feet. I'd never moved from my place before, when my father was telling a story. I always felt rooted to the spot. But this was different. The story seemed to be slipping out of his grasp and into ours: mine and Ferdinand's.

We came face to face, stretched out our arms and clasped hands, and looked into each other's eyes.

After that I didn't notice much of what was happening, though I could hear my father still telling the story to himself. For a while, he was talking about the other people who had been on the ship, the wicked brother who had dispossessed the King of Naples (he meant his own brother, of course). He said that now that this man was on the island, there was no knowing what harm might come. Anyone – my father included – might get murdered, and there was also Caliban to think of, because he was always looking for a chance to stir up trouble in people's minds.

Out of the corner of my eye, I could see figures coming and going. The people who had been on the ship: bad men and good, drunk men and sober; sometimes quarrelling and fighting, sometimes agreeing and making friends. All the time I had a sense that this was going to be the last story of all, and that it was coming to an end, and that I didn't need to listen to it any more. I didn't need to hear any stories told by my father now, because something had happened which had released me from the enchantment of his tales; and if he went on telling them, I would no longer be there to hear them.

I saw him getting to his feet, and holding out his arms like a magician, and the broken ship somehow mended itself, and came sailing right up to the shore, and everyone climbed on board – they were all the best of friends now. I even thought I saw Ariel and Caliban, whom I'd never even glimpsed before, but had only heard about. I thought that my father was waving goodbye to them, leaving them on the island, and that the island itself was starting to fade away.

The ship was beginning to move and, suddenly, I realized that Ferdinand and I, still holding each other's hands and looking into each other's eyes, were on board with everyone else. We could scarcely see the island now.

And where was my father? I thought I remembered him saying that he had climbed on the ship too, and was coming back with us, maybe to reclaim his rightful kingdom. But somehow I felt he was still on the island, if there really was an island; or maybe that he had simply stopped telling stories for ever. I thought I heard his voice saying, gently: 'The end. And I mean really the end, Miranda, of any story that I can tell you. Go and tell your own stories now.'

And Ferdinand and I looked at each other, and we began to tell ourselves the best story that we had ever heard; and we are still telling it today.